Dates of a Decade

THE 1950s

Paul Harrison

with additional text by Jacqueline Laks Gorman

ARCTURUS

This edition first published by Arcturus Publishing
Distributed by Black Rabbit Books
123 South Broad Street
Mankato
Minnesota MN 56001

Copyright © 2009 Arcturus Publishing Limited

Printed in the United States

All rights reserved

Series concept: Alex Woolf
Editor and picture researcher: Alex Woolf
U.S. editor: Jacqueline Laks Gorman
Designer: Phipps Design

Library of Congress Cataloging-in-Publication Data

Harrison, Paul, 1969-
  The 1950s / Paul Harrison.
    p. cm. -- (Dates of a decade)
  Includes index.
  ISBN 978-1-84837-281-8 (hardcover)
  1. History, Modern--1945-1989--Juvenile literature. I. Title.

D842.5.H377 2010
909.82'5--dc22
                                    2009000005

Contents

GLOBAL EVENTS

UNITED STATES EVENTS

The McCarthy Witch Hunts

Soon after the end of World War II (1939–1945), tensions began to rise between the United States and the communist Soviet Union and their respective allies. Each side believed the other was trying to overthrow its government and replace it with a government that supported its own, opposing ideology. This conflict was known as the Cold War, since no direct military engagements took place between the main opponents, although the threat of an all-out nuclear conflict was always there.

In February 1950, at the height of Cold War anxiety, an American politician from the Republican Party, Senator Joseph McCarthy, stood up to make a speech in Wheeling, West Virginia, and tapped right into the nightmares of the American people – he claimed that the U.S. government itself had been infiltrated by communist spies.

"Communists in the government"

In his speech, McCarthy began by painting a grim picture of how the United States was outnumbered by the communist powers to the east. Then he made a dramatic claim: "I have here in my hand a list of 205 … a list of names that were made known to the Secretary of State as being members of the Communist Party and who nevertheless are still working and shaping policy in the State Department."

The papers ran the story and public fears were whipped up, especially because McCarthy continued to make his allegations despite never providing substantial proof. Eleven days later, Senator McCarthy gave a six-hour speech to Congress where he identified over 80 people – though not by name – who he claimed were communist sympathizers. Again he supplied little proof, but despite this the story struck a chord and won popular support.

Joseph McCarthy is seen here in typically belligerent style during an appearance at a Senate investigation into communist infiltration in the State Department in March 1950.

Interrogating suspects

Partly as a result of McCarthy's actions, the Republicans won the presidential election in 1952. Afterward, McCarthy was made chairman of the Committee on Government Operations and began to interrogate suspected communists in many areas of American life. Politicians and academics were hounded from office; journalists, writers, film-makers, and actors were blacklisted (shunned by their profession), and people from all walks of life were persecuted if they were even suspected of having left-wing views. Colleague testified against colleague at special hearings set up to root out communist sympathizers.

However, McCarthy's reign of terror lasted only until 1954. He met his match when trying to get an army officer, Captain Irving Peress, court-martialed for alleged "un-American" attitudes. McCarthy failed, and the U.S. public, tired of seeing America fighting with itself, turned against the senator. He was relieved of his position soon afterward.

McCarthy was always big news. Here he is surrounded by journalists in a lunch break during a hearing in September 1954.

What the papers said

Senator Joseph R. McCarthy … asserted that spies had been planted in the State Department to shape the policy of our government and rob this nation of its potency…. Sen. McCarthy brought gasps from some members of his audience and there were tears in the eyes of others as he made his case.

The Reno Evening Gazette, February 13, 1950

- **SEE ALSO**
  Pages 6–7: June 25, 1950: The Korean War Begins

- **FURTHER INFORMATION**
  📖 Books:
  Snapshots in History: McCarthyism: The Red Scare by Brian Fitzgerald (Compass Point, 2006)
  Websites:
  historymatters.gmu.edu/d/6456
  McCarthy's Wheeling speech

25
JUNE
1950

The Korean War Begins

By the end of World War II, the country of Korea was split in two along a line known as the 38th parallel. The Soviet army occupied the north and the Americans the south. Originally, elections had been planned to unite the country, but in the climate of mistrust that existed between the United States and the Soviet Union, these elections never took place and the country remained divided. In 1948, governments were set up in each country. The communists took control of the north under the rule of Kim Il Sung, while in the south, Syngman Rhee and his anti-communist government were elected to power.

General MacArthur (in the black jacket) inspects facilities at Inchon on September 16, 1950, the day after UN forces landed there.

Invasion

In 1950, with the new South Korean government established, the American troops left. Then, during the early hours of June 25, North Korea invaded the South in an attempt to reunite Korea by force. The North Korean advance was rapid and the army quickly overran the South Korean capital of Seoul. At this stage it appeared that the North would completely occupy the South.

The Americans, already concerned at the prospect of communist expansion in Southeast Asia, were quick to respond. Troops were immediately dispatched and assistance was sought from the United Nations (UN) on the grounds that a democratically elected government was being overthrown by force. The UN agreed to help and the U.S. forces were joined by troops sent from Britain, Australia, and other Western countries. The UN forces, under the command of U.S. General Douglas MacArthur, landed at a place called Inchon, in occupied territory, on September 15, 1950, and proceeded to force back the North Koreans beyond the 38th parallel.

Counterattack

The goal of liberating South Korea had been achieved. But the easy victory encouraged the Americans – with UN approval – to continue the fight with the aim of reuniting Korea under the government of Syngman Rhee. The UN forces took the North Korean capital, Pyongyang, on October 19, 1950.

A wounded American soldier is carried to safety by his comrades during a battle in July 1953.

However, just as it looked as if the UN forces would completely occupy North Korea, China came to the aid of its communist neighbor. Together, China and North Korea mounted a counter-offensive that forced the UN forces into retreat, and Seoul fell once more on January 4, 1951.

The UN forces rallied and advanced northward again, until a stalemate was reached in the autumn of 1951. Eventually a ceasefire was reached at midnight on July 27, 1953 and the border was set near the 38th parallel, where it had been originally. The two countries are still technically at war today and an uneasy ceasefire remains.

- **SEE ALSO**
  Pages 4–5: February 9, 1950:
  The McCarthy Witch Hunts

- **FURTHER INFORMATION**
  📖 Books:
  Atlas of Conflicts: The Korean War by Reg Grant (Franklin Watts, 2004)
  🖱 Websites:
  www.historycentral.com/korea/index.html
  Major events of the Korean War

What the papers said

The outbreak of hostilities in Korea is particularly serious in the world's eyes because the two contending armies are so akin to their foster parents, the Soviet Union and the United States.

The New York Times, June 26, 1950

22 JANUARY 1952

The First Commercial Jet Airliner

When passengers at London's Heathrow Airport boarded the British Overseas Aircraft Corporation's plane, G-ALYP, they were more than usually excited. Air travel was still an activity of the wealthy, but this history-making flight was about to change all that; this was the maiden flight of the de Havilland Comet, the world's first commercial jet airliner.

A new era

Jet-powered aircraft were first developed during World War II, but until 1952 had been used for fighter aircraft, not passenger planes. Commercial air travel had relied on propeller-driven planes that were slow, noisy, and expensive. The Comet's sleek, modern lines heralded a new era of speed and comfort. The plane was capable of carrying up to 44 passengers, which was actually fewer than some of its propeller-driven rivals, but it had a top speed of almost 500 miles per hour (800 kilometres per hour), which was nearly twice as fast as most of the competition.

The first passengers board the BOAC Comet for its maiden flight from London Heathrow to Johannesburg.

The sleek lines of the Comet, combined with its revolutionary jet engines, heralded the future of commercial air travel.

This cutting-edge technology was beyond the means of most people. The Comet was initially used for the prestigious London-to-Johannesburg route, and its passengers all tended to be very wealthy. Today, an airplane could travel this distance directly, but the Comet required refueling stops at Rome, Beirut, Khartoum, Entebbe, and Livingstone. The whole journey took around 23 hours.

Design flaw

Disaster was to strike the Comet, though. A serious design flaw caused the cabin walls to give way around the windows. This resulted in a number of fatal crashes in 1953 and 1954, and the entire fleet of planes was grounded in 1954. The Comet flew again in 1958 but was forever tainted by the tragedies that had befallen it earlier that decade.

In its brief career, however, the Comet did point the way forward for air travel. Other manufacturers were quick to see the advantages of commercial jet airliners, and as faster and bigger planes were built, ticket prices dropped. The Comet that took off that January morning in 1952 represented the first step on the road to mass air travel.

eye witness

There's no real impression of speed while you are in the air, it's only when you flash by an occasional cloud that there's any real impression of movement. For most of the time it's like being suspended in space, with the clouds far below and the sky in daytime a deeper blue because of the height. It's quieter than the normal passenger airplane and it's quite easy to carry on a conversation.

Douglas Willis, a passenger on the maiden flight.
Quoted from news.bbc.co.uk/onthisday/hi/dates/
stories/may/2/newsid_2480000/2480339.stm

- **SEE ALSO**
  Pages 34–35: October 4, 1957: Sputnik Is Launched

- **FURTHER INFORMATION**
  Books:
  De Havilland Comet by Kev Darling (Crowood Press, 2005)
  Websites:
  www.rafmuseum.org.uk/cosford/exhibitions/comet/index.cfm
  For interesting photographs of the Comet and its problems

DNA Is Discovered

It was a damp February day when the young scientists Francis Crick and James Watson walked into the Eagle pub (bar) in Cambridge, UK, for some lunch. They often ate there after working in their nearby laboratory. However, today was no ordinary day. They had made a discovery that morning that would revolutionize the world of science and medicine. "We have found the secret of life," announced Crick as they entered the pub. He was not far wrong.

The code of life

What Crick and Watson had found was the structure of a macromolecule (a tiny amount of a chemical substance) called deoxyribonucleic acid – or DNA. DNA is important because it contains the genetic code for life. In other words, it determines how a living thing will grow and what it will look like. For example, it is through our DNA that we inherit characteristics from our parents, whether it is the color of our hair or the height we will grow. DNA is what makes oak trees look like oak trees or ladybugs like ladybugs.

Scientists had known what DNA did and were pretty sure of what it was made of, but significantly they had no idea of how it was made or what it looked like. This is what Crick and Watson set out to discover. Instead of conducting experiments like other scientists, they spent time imagining what they thought it *should* look like. They thought it would probably be a double helix with molecules in between – essentially, they believed it would look something like a twisted ladder. What they needed now was proof.

Nobel Prize

Their breakthrough came when they were shown an image from a special kind of X-ray, which supported their idea. Crick and Watson published

⊙ eye witness

We wish to suggest a structure for the salt of deoxyribose nucleic acid (DNA). This structure has novel features which are of considerable biological interest…. A structure for nucleic acid has already been proposed by Pauling and Corey. They kindly made their manuscript available to us in advance of publication. Their model consists of three intertwined chains, with the phosphates near the fibre axis, and the bases on the outside. In our opinion, this structure is unsatisfactory…. We wish to put forward a radically different structure for the salt of deoxyribose nucleic acid. This structure has two helical chains each coiled around the same axis….

Quoted from the letter Crick and Watson published in *Nature*, April 25, 1953

their findings in *Nature* magazine, but not many people understood the significance of the breakthrough at first. As other scientists found evidence that corroborated Crick and Watson's theory, interest gradually grew. The pair were eventually awarded a Nobel Prize in 1962 for their discovery.

There was some controversy over the award. The X-ray image they had seen belonged to a scientist named Rosalind Franklin. She was also studying DNA and she had not personally given permission for Crick and Watson to see the image. She died at the age of 37 in 1958 without really being given the credit that she deserved for her part in the discovery.

James Watson (left) and Francis Crick inspect their model of the structure of DNA at their laboratory in Cambridge.

- **SEE ALSO**
  Pages 18–19: December 23, 1954:
  The First Organ Transplant

- **FURTHER INFORMATION**
  📖 Books:
  Genes and DNA by Anna Claybourne
  (Usborne, 2003)
  🖱 Websites:
  library.thinkquest.org/20830/Textbook/
  HistoryofDNAResearch.htm
  A brief history of DNA research

Stalin Dies

After four days in a coma following a massive stroke, Joseph Stalin, General Secretary of the Communist Party and leader of the Soviet Union, died. He had controlled the communist world with an iron fist for a quarter of a century and was feared equally at home and abroad. His death appeared to promise a new era for the entire world.

Rise to power

It had been quite a journey for Stalin. He was a Georgian, not a Russian, born in 1879 and christened Josef Vissarionovich Dzhugashvili. He had an unconventional upbringing. As a child, he suffered beatings by his father and was later expelled from a seminary (a training school for priests) for studying the works of Karl Marx. He became a revolutionary with the communist Bolshevik party and edited their paper, *Pravda*.

In October 1917, a revolution brought the communists to power in Russia. All the states that had been under Russian control joined with Russia to form the Union of Soviet Socialist Republics (USSR), or the Soviet Union. Stalin was appointed General Secretary of the Communist Party in 1922. Two years later, the Soviet leader, Vladimir Lenin, died. Stalin used his position to create a strong power base within the party and to destroy his rivals, enabling him to become absolute ruler of the Soviet Union by 1928.

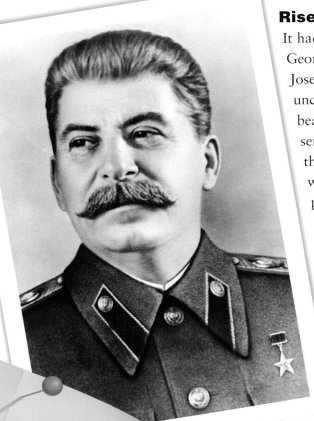

This official portrait of Joseph Stalin dates from around 1940.

How it was reported

The Central Committee ... announce with deep grief to the party and all workers that on March 5 at 9.50 P.M., Josef Vissarionovich Stalin died after a serious illness. The heart of the collaborator and follower of the genius of Lenin's work, the wise leader and teacher of the Communist party and of the Soviet people, stopped beating.

Moscow Home Service, March 7, 1953

Stalin's rule

Stalin led the Soviet Union with a mixture of charisma and fear. He could be an inspirational leader, and he turned a primarily agricultural nation into an industrial superpower. But this came at a terrible cost: conditions both in the cities and in the countryside were grim, and many people starved. During the 1930s, Stalin executed millions of people and imprisoned millions more in slave labor camps, claiming they were enemies of the state. He displayed a similar indifference to peoples' lives during World War II. Although his Red Army eventually defeated the invading Germans, the Soviet Union suffered more casualties than every other combatant nation combined, partly due to the tactics Stalin encouraged.

After the war, Stalin succumbed to increasing paranoia, and the arrests and imprisonments continued until his death. Many Soviet citizens mourned Stalin's passing, despite his monstrous deeds. They believed in his ideals and were proud that he had made the Soviet Union a great world power. However, a large number of people were secretly relieved. It is estimated that under Stalin's leadership, around 20 million Soviet citizens were executed, 18 million were sent to slave labor camps, and another 10 million were deported. Three years after his death, Stalin's successor, Nikita Khrushchev, made a speech denouncing what Stalin had done.

Soviet factory workers gather around a radio to hear the announcement of Stalin's death.

- **SEE ALSO**
  Pages 28–29: November 4, 1956:
  The Hungarian Uprising Is Crushed

- **FURTHER INFORMATION**
  Books:
  20th Century Leaders: Joseph Stalin
  by Peter Chrisp (Wayland, 2002)
  Websites:
  www.channel4.com/history/microsites/H/history/n-s/stalin.html
  Good overview of Stalin's career, with source material

Everest Is Conquered

As Edmund Hillary and Tenzing Norgay ate breakfast by their tents on a clear dawn near the top of Mount Everest, they knew the day would end either in triumph or intense disappointment. Months of planning and weeks of trekking lay behind them. Further down the mountain was the rest of the expedition that John Hunt had organized to make an attempt on the summit. Ahead of them in the snow were the footprints of the team that had tried and failed to reach the summit just three days earlier. If Hillary and Tenzing also failed, the team would most likely have to return home as the bad monsoon weather was closing in. This was their last chance.

The roof of the world

Mount Everest is the highest mountain in the world. It sits among the Himalayan mountain range in Nepal and rises 29,035 feet (8,840 meters). Its height was first calculated by surveyors working for Britain in 1854. The surveyors called the mountain Peak XV. It was later named after the man who organized the survey, Sir George Everest. The Nepalese themselves call the mountain Chomolungma. Whatever its name, the

Mount Everest, the highest mountain in the world. Hillary and Tenzing approached the summit from the left of the peak.

mountain is a dangerous place of avalanches, high winds, severe storms and, in its upper areas, little oxygen. It had never been climbed. Many had tried but all had failed, and some did not live to tell the tale.

The expedition leader, John Hunt, was meticulous in his preparations. He assembled a large team of 13 climbers and doctors, as well as a team of Sherpas – local people who lived near the foot of Everest – who helped carry the equipment. Hunt's team also used the most up-to-date technology, including oxygen cylinders to help the climbers breathe at high altitudes. Now, 102 days after leaving Britain, the success or failure of the expedition had come down to the abilities of two climbers – and luck.

Reaching the summit

For Hillary and Tenzing, the final stage of the climb was grueling. It was made more difficult by an enormous lump of rock and snow that they had to squirm up like a chimney – all this while carrying oxygen tanks and wrapped in multiple layers of clothing. Finally, at 11.30 A.M., Hillary and Tenzing made it – they had reached the highest point on earth.

They spent only 15 minutes on the summit as they needed to return to camp before their oxygen ran out. There were no satellite phones in the 1950s, so it was days before the news of their triumph reached the outside world.

Tenzing Norgay (left) and Edmund Hillary relax at their camp at Thyangboche, Nepal, following their successful climb to the summit of Everest.

⊙ eye witness

Far from failure, this was IT! They had made it!! Feelings welled up uncontrollably as I now quickened my pace.... The next moment I was with them: handshakes – even I blush to say, hugs – for the triumphant pair. A special one for Tenzing, so well merited for him personally, this victory, both for himself and for his people.

John Hunt in his book *The Ascent of Everest* (London Readers Union, 1955)

- **SEE ALSO**
  Pages 16–17: May 6, 1954: Breaking the Four-Minute Mile

- **FURTHER INFORMATION**
  📖 Books:
  DK Eyewitness: Everest (DK Publishing, 2001)
  🖱 Websites:
  Imagingeverest.rgs.org/Concepts/Virtual_Everest/-75.html
  For information on Everest and all the Everest expeditions, from the Royal Geographical Society

Breaking the Four-Minute Mile

It was a blustery day at the cinder race track at Iffley Road in Oxford, UK. The event was the annual competition between Oxford University and the Amateur Athletics Association (AAA). However, this year was to be a little bit special. Roger Bannister, a 25-year-old runner from the AAA and former student of Oxford University, was trying to accomplish one of the greatest feats in athletics history – he was going to try to run a mile in under four minutes.

Careful preparation

Although a number of runners had come close to breaking the four-minute barrier, no one had yet managed it. This led many people to believe that it was physically impossible. Bannister had other ideas. He knew that preparation was key. To help him, he arranged for there to be two pacemakers – athletes who would set the pace for Bannister by running for

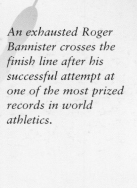

An exhausted Roger Bannister crosses the finish line after his successful attempt at one of the most prized records in world athletics.

as long as possible at record-breaking pace. He would run behind them, then take over for the last section of the race as the pacemakers tired. The pacemakers were Chris Brasher and Chris Chataway.

On the day of the competition it was quite windy – hardly ideal conditions for a record-breaking run – and the attempt was almost called off. However, the wind dropped slightly as the race was about to begin, and Bannister decided to try for the record. A false start added to the already tense atmosphere. The athletes were pulled back for a restart, much to Bannister's annoyance as he was worried that the wind would pick up again.

The miracle mile

When the race finally got underway, the first pacemaker, Chris Brasher, maintained the perfect pace to break the record. The first half mile was completed in 1 minute 58 seconds, and shortly afterward the second pacemaker, Chris Chataway, moved past Bannister and Brasher to take up the lead. He also did a brilliant job. Around 220 yards (200 metres) from the finish line, Bannister himself moved into the lead. This was the best chance anyone had had to break the record and Bannister was not about to throw it away. To the roars of the 3,000 spectators, he found a final burst of energy and crossed the line in a time of 3 minutes 59.4 seconds – immediately collapsing into the arms of a friend.

Bannister's magnificent achievement is regarded as one of the greatest moments in sports history. His record was broken the very next month by the Australian runner John Landy, and Bannister himself retired from racing by the end of the year to pursue his medical studies. But he had cemented his place in history as the man who ran the "miracle mile."

⦿ eye witness

It was the most memorable race I ever ran and I remember all the details. I knew the record attempt was on because Bannister asked me to keep out of his way on the first two laps.... It was an exhilarating night and I was proud to have taken part in such a historic race.

Tom Hulatt, who came third in the race. Quoted in www.tommyhulatt.org.uk/

What the papers said

The dream of world athletes through the years was achieved yesterday by an Englishman – 25-year-old Roger Bannister, who became the first man on earth to run a mile in under four minutes. His feat at Oxford last evening – against a 20-mile-an-hour cross-wind was equal in dramatic achievement to the crashing of the sound barrier in the air.

Daily Express, May 7, 1954

• **SEE ALSO**
Pages 14–15: May 29, 1953:
Everest Is Conquered

• **FURTHER INFORMATION**
Books:
The First Four Minutes by Roger Bannister
(Sutton Publishing, 2004)
Websites:
www.cbc.ca/ideas/features/four_minute/
index.html
Roger Bannister recalls the race in his own words

The First Organ Transplant

It was two days before Christmas when 23-year-old Ronald Herrick gave his twin brother Richard an early and most unusual present. For Richard, who was dying of a kidney disease, it was probably the best present he could have received. Ronald donated one of his own kidneys in order to give his brother the best chance of survival. Now Richard had to undergo a very risky surgical procedure: the transplant of a major organ.

Overcoming rejection

Organ transplants had been tried before but had never worked. The body of the transplant recipient always rejected the new organ. The body's immune system (defense mechanism) regarded the new organ as something foreign to itself and therefore harmful, and attacked it. Doctors needed to find some way of convincing the immune system that the new organ was not foreign.

Joseph Murray, the surgeon who was to perform the operation, had good reason to believe that this time things would be different. Richard and Ronald were identical twins – they had come from same egg – so biologically they were very similar. Consequently, the immune system might not recognize the new kidney as being foreign.

However, there was an ethical issue that had to be addressed before the operation could be performed. By taking a kidney from Ronald, the surgical team could be seen as contravening a doctor's duty not to cause harm to a patient. Some people were not even sure a person could live with one kidney. The members of the surgical team were convinced, however, that Ronald would be fine and that the operation was ethical.

Richard Herrick (seated) is pushed from the Peter Bent Brigham Hospital in Boston, Massachusetts, by his twin brother Ronald following their successful kidney transplant.

 eye witness

We didn't think we made history, we didn't even think of history. We thought we were going to save a patient.

Joseph Murray, quoted in www.npr.org/templates/story/story.php?storyId=4233669

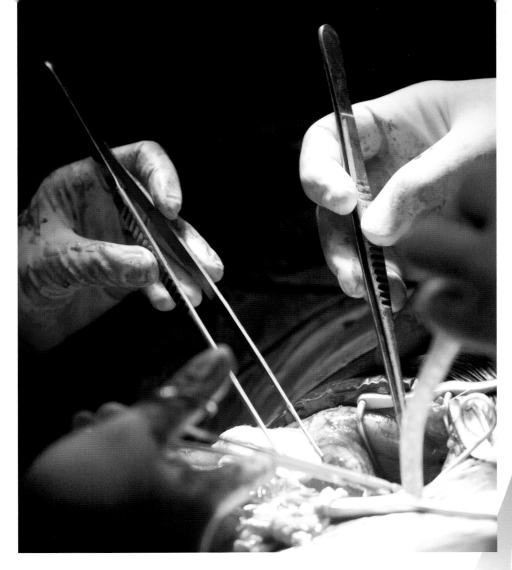

Surgeons at work during a modern kidney transplant operation.

The operation

Murray knew he had just one chance at the operation – after all, Ronald had only one spare kidney – so Murray organized a trial run using a dead body. He wanted to be sure that he knew exactly what he was doing when the real operation began.

The real operation started at 8.15 A.M. and lasted for over three hours. First, the healthy kidney had to be removed from Ronald. When this was done, the more difficult procedure of attaching it to Richard was carried out. Fortunately, everything went smoothly, much to the relief of all concerned.

Richard Herrick's body did not reject the kidney, but he lived only another eight years. Nevertheless, the operation was a great success for its time and paved the way for more successful organ transplants in the future. Ronald Herrick lived into his 70s.

- **SEE ALSO**
  Pages 10–11: February 28, 1953:
  DNA Is discovered

- **FURTHER INFORMATION**
  Books:
  Cutting Edge Medicine: Organ Transplantation
  by Carol Ballard (Franklin Watts, 2007)
  Websites:
  www.hno.harvard.edu/gazette/2001/10.04/
  11-murray.html
  For a profile of Joseph Murray

The First McDonald's Franchise Opens

Ray Kroc had always had an eye for a business opportunity. The problem was that a real opportunity had never come his way before. During the early 1950s he worked as a salesman, marketing milkshake mixers across the United States. He was on a routine visit to one of his customers in California when Kroc saw his chance. His customers were two brothers who owned and ran a hamburger and milkshake restaurant. The business was doing so well they were running eight of Kroc's milkshake mixers all day long. The restaurant was called McDonald's.

Ray Kroc, the man who turned McDonald's from a single fast-food restaurant into a global phenomenon.

A winning formula

What made the McDonald brothers' operation stand out was its simplicity. Their restaurant had no tables and chairs and their utensils were made of plastic. The menu was limited, offering around nine different items, and it was cheap: a hamburger cost only 15 cents. However, the biggest selling point of the business was that it was quick: a hamburger took under a minute to prepare and hand over to the customer. The restaurant offered fast food for people in a hurry.

Ray Kroc could envisage thousands of McDonald's restaurants right across the country. He tried to sell the idea to the brothers, Dick and Mac, but they weren't convinced. They had already sold some franchises – the right of other businesses to use their name – and hadn't made any money. Besides, they didn't have the time or energy to run a major franchising operation. Kroc, however, did. He offered to set up the franchises and pay the brothers a small share of the profits. They agreed, and in April 1955, Kroc opened the first of the new McDonald's franchises in Des Plaines, Illinois.

⊙ eye witness

A chocolate malt. I had two hamburgers and french fries. And hamburgers were 15 cents a piece? Something like that, right. I think it was 53 cents for the whole meal.

Glen Volkman, one of the first McDonald's customers. Quoted in abclocal.go.com/wls/story?section= News&id=2973642

The original McDonald's in Des Plaines no longer exists, but a replica has been built further down the street and houses the McDonald's Museum.

Kroc's master stroke

Kroc stayed true to the McDonald brothers' methods. He kept the same limited menu and cheap prices. The Des Plaines business was a success, and by the end of 1956 there were 13 other McDonald's around the country. Kroc's master stroke was to make all of the restaurants identical. They would serve the same food cooked in the same way for the same price, and they would all be clean – Kroc was rightly obsessed with the idea that people like clean restaurants.

It was a winning formula. By the end of the decade there were over 200 McDonald's across the midwest and western United States. By 1970 there were over 1,500, including 50 in Canada. Kroc was a wealthy man. The McDonald brothers were also rich, though not as rich as they might have been. Kroc, ever the businessman, had persuaded the brothers to sell him their rights in the business for $2.7 million in 1963. In 1965, Kroc's stake in the business was worth $32 million. And the company kept on growing. Today, there are over 20,000 McDonald's restaurants in some 100 countries around the world.

eye witness

I grew up in Des Plaines. I was only 6 years old in 1955 but a bit later I remember some adults giving their opinion that it is "just a passing fad." So much for that thought! Later, when I was in college, during a couple of summers, I was a substitute mail carrier for the Post Office. Often, I would get the route that included this restaurant (at the time it was still an operating restaurant) and I would stop in to have a Coke or if at lunch time, probably something to eat.

Unknown McDonald's customer. Quoted on www.waymarking.com/wm/details.aspx?f=1&guid =7a495d16-e89e-48f6-ae99-18420986253d&gid=4

- **SEE ALSO**
  Pages 38–39: March 9, 1959:
  Barbie Is Launched

- **FURTHER INFORMATION**
  Books:
  Lives and Times: Ray Kroc
  (Heinemann, 2003)
  Websites:
  www.mcdonalds.ca/en/aboutus/history.aspx
  For a detailed history

30
SEPTEMBER
1955

James Dean Dies

James Dean seemingly had it all. He was young, good-looking, and was experiencing a meteoric rise to fame. He had just finished shooting his latest film, *Giant*, and was now off to take part in the other love of his life, auto racing. He and his mechanic were heading to Salinas, California, where Dean was due to race. They would never get there. An oncoming car turned into the path of Dean's Porsche Spyder. The driver was apparently unable to see the silver sports car in the twilight. The two cars met head on and Dean's Porsche was sent hurtling into a ditch. Dean was dead before the ambulance could get him to the hospital.

Rising star

James Byron Dean was born on February 8, 1931 in Marion, Indiana. When he was 19, he studied acting at the James Whitmore acting workshop, and went on to study drama at the University of California, Los Angeles. He left his university course part way through in 1951 to pursue his acting career. Dean appeared in a number of television shows and theater productions, but only made three major motion pictures. They were all filmed over a period of about 12 months in 1954 and 1955 and catapulted Dean into the major league of film stars.

James Dean in his iconic sports jacket and white tee-shirt.

The first film he appeared in was *East of Eden*. It was directed by Elia Kazan, one of the main informants during the McCarthy witch-hunts. However, Dean really made his mark in the films *Rebel Without a Cause* and *Giant*. Dean would never know the enormous impact he would make with these films since they were released after his death.

A love of speed

Dean seemed to epitomize the "live fast, die young" mentality, with his dynamic and unpredictable acting style and his part-time motor-racing career. He raced three times and did very well, finishing second in one of the races. It was often suspected that Dean's love of speed contributed to his accident. But although it was true that he had been stopped for speeding earlier on that fateful night, analysis of the crash site carried out in 2005 suggests that Dean's car had been traveling below the speed limit at the time of the accident.

The fact that Dean died young, just as his career was taking off, undoubtedly contributed to his fame. He would never grow old or star in bad films, and he would always be the good-looking, edgy actor who died too soon. Dean's legacy was immediate. He became the first actor to be nominated for an Academy Award after he had died. In fact, he received not one but two posthumous nominations, for his roles in *East of Eden* and *Giant*.

The mangled remains of Dean's Porsche Spyder lie by the side of the road at the scene of the accident. Remarkably, Dean's passenger, Rolf Wutherich, survived the crash.

What the papers said

James Dean, 24, one of Hollywood's brightest new motion-picture stars, was killed early last night in a head-on collision at the rural town of Cholame, about 19 miles east of Paso Robles.... The young actor met death in his German-built Porsche sports car while en route to road races at Salinas.... Under contract to Warner Brothers studios, the intense young star frequently had been compared to Marlon Brando and both were products of director Elia Kazan's school for tyro actors.

Los Angeles Times, October 1, 1955

- **SEE ALSO**
  Pages 30–31: January 6, 1957: Elvis is Censored

- **FURTHER INFORMATION**
  Books:
  American Rebels: James Dean: Dream as If You'll Live Forever by Karen Clemens Warrick (Enslow Publishers, 2006)

  Websites:
  www.jamesdean.com/
  The official James Dean website

Rosa Parks Refuses to Change Seats

By the 1950s, slavery had been abolished in the United States for almost 100 years. Despite this, African Americans continued to suffer discrimination in the southern states. In the town of Montgomery, Alabama, for example, black Americans were not allowed to mix with whites in many public places, including public transportation. On Montgomery's buses, African Americans had to sit in the back half of the bus – and even then, if the front half was full, they were expected to give up their seats for whites. As no black person was allowed to sit in the same row as a white person, up to four black people were often forced to give up their seats for the sake of a single white person.

Arrest and trial

On the evening of December 1, 1955, Rosa Parks, a 42-year-old African American, was returning from work in Montgomery. The bus was full and she and the other people in her row were asked to move so a white person could sit down. After some grumbling, three people got up, but Rosa Parks, burning with the injustice of it all, quietly but firmly refused. The bus driver had her arrested, and she was put on trial on December 5.

Rosa Parks sitting at the front of a bus in Montgomery, Alabama, after segregation was ruled illegal by the Supreme Court.

Parks's arrest caused an uproar. Various groups quickly mobilized, including the Women's Political Council (WPC), which represented African American professional women, and the National Association for the Advancement of Colored People, a group set up to promote equality. At her trial, Parks was found guilty and fined $14. On the same day, the WPC organized a bus boycott, and a group called the Montgomery Improvement Association (MIA) was set up to challenge Montgomery's segregation policy.

Bus boycott

The boycott lasted for 381 days and was widely supported by much of Montgomery's black population. Instead of catching buses, they shared taxis or walked to work. The boycott was only lifted after the Supreme Court ruled that segregation was unconstitutional. The ruling may well have been a relief to the bus company, too, as it had suffered financially from losing a large percentage of its passengers.

The civil rights movement (the movement that aimed to abolish discrimination against African Americans) had scored an important victory. One principled woman had stood up to an unfair system and won. It was also a triumph for the MIA and raised the profile of its leader, a little-known Baptist minister named Martin Luther King, who would go on to become the most famous leader of the American civil rights movement.

Rosa Parks lost her job as a result of her political battle and was forced to move away from Montgomery in 1957 after receiving death threats. This did not dissuade her from continuing to play an active part in the civil rights movement. In 1987, Parks established the Rosa and Raymond Parks Institute for Self-Development, which encourages young people to further their education and life skills, as well as learning about the civil rights movement.

What the papers said

The arrest of a Negro who refused to move to the colored section of a city bus may bring a court test of segregated transportation in the cradle of the Confederacy. While thousands of other Negroes boycotted Montgomery City Lines in protest, Mrs. Rosa Parks was fined $14 in police court yesterday for disregarding a driver's order to move to the rear of a bus last Thursday.

Associated Press, December 6, 1955

eye witness

Oh, she's so sweet. They've messed with the wrong one now!

Unnamed woman in court on seeing Rosa Parks. Quoted on www.time.com/time/time100/heroes/profile/parks03.html

- **FURTHER INFORMATION**
- Books:
  Rosa Parks by Camilla Wilson (Scholastic, 2001)
- Websites:
  www.rosaparks.org/index.html
  For information on the work of the Rosa and Raymond Parks Institute
  www.time.com/time/time100/heroes/profile/parks01.html
  For a good profile of Rosa Parks

The Suez Crisis Begins

The Suez Canal links the Red Sea with the Mediterranean Sea and provides an important access route for ships traveling between Europe and Asia that would otherwise need to sail around Africa. The canal, which cuts through Egyptian territory, was constructed by a French company between 1858 and 1869, and was then owned and operated by mainly British and French shareholders on a 99-year lease from Egypt. The canal proved to be of immense strategic and financial value for the British and French.

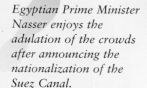

Egyptian Prime Minister Nasser enjoys the adulation of the crowds after announcing the nationalization of the Suez Canal.

Nasser's action

In the early 1950s, as Cold War tensions rose around the world, Egypt decided to ally itself with the Soviet Union rather than with the Western powers, partly because of the West's support for Egypt's enemy, Israel. In retaliation, Britain and the United States withdrew promised funding for

Egypt's Aswan Dam project. Egypt's leader, General Gamal Abdel Nasser, responded by declaring, on July 26, that he would nationalize (place under state control) the Suez Canal. He claimed that the revenue raised from the canal would pay for the dam within five years. Nasser's action triggered what became known as the Suez Crisis.

Invasion

Britain and France were outraged. They secretly agreed with Israel to invade Egypt, hoping to secure the canal and possibly cause the overthrow of Nasser. The plan was for Israel to invade first. Britain and France would then send in troops and instruct the Israeli and Egyptian armies to withdraw to a distance of 10 miles (16 kilometers) from either side of the canal.

An Anglo-French force would then take control of the area around the canal. On October 29, Israel invaded Egypt, and two days later Britain and France started a bombing campaign, followed shortly afterward by an invasion.

The superpowers intervene

This action angered both superpowers. The Soviet Union threatened to join forces with Egypt, and the United States, far from coming to its former allies' aid, was highly critical of the invasion. The U.S. government threatened to sell its reserves of the British pound, thereby causing a collapse of the British currency. The invasion also prompted some Arab countries to impose an oil embargo on Britain and France.

Britain, France, and Israel were forced to remove their troops, which were replaced by a United Nations peacekeeping force. The British prime minister, Sir Anthony Eden, resigned as a result of the fiasco. The crisis served as an important lesson for the former world powers, Britain and France, that real power now lay with the United States and Soviet Union.

An Egyptian boy stands amid the rubble of ruined buildings at Port Said, Egypt. A British tank can be seen in the background.

What the papers said

Gamal Abdel Nasser's seizure of the Suez Canal can plunge the Middle East into a crisis as deep as any it has known since World War II.

If Egypt gets away with it Nasser may emerge eventually as the master of the Middle East. If he loses this gamble he can wind up on the rubbish heap of former dictators…. If developments should bring about a situation in which the canal were closed, this surely would lead to some kind of military action throwing the entire Arab World into a panic.

Associated Press, July 27, 1956

- **FURTHER INFORMATION**
- Books:
  War and Conflict in the Middle East: The Suez Crisis by James W. Fiscus (Rosen Publishing, 2004)
- Websites:
  www.spartacus.schoolnet.co.uk/COLDsuez.htm
  Contains interesting source material
  news.bbc.co.uk/1/hi/world/middle_east/5195068.stm
  For clear maps

The Hungarian Uprising Is Crushed

After World War II, Hungary, like the other countries of Eastern Europe, became a communist state, politically and economically dependent on the Soviet Union. Encouraged by the Soviet leadership, the Hungarian government became increasingly repressive, imprisoning and executing thousands of political opponents. After the death of Stalin in 1953 and the "destalinization" process introduced by his successor Khrushchev, many communist states hoped that Soviet control would decrease.

Students in Budapest defiantly fly the Hungarian flag and brandish weapons during the uprising.

Demonstrations

In Hungary, a series of anti-Soviet demonstrations by students quickly escalated into full-blown riots that threatened to topple the government. On October 23, the government requested Soviet military assistance. Soviet tanks entered the Hungarian capital Budapest the following day. At the same time, a more popular leader, Imre Nagy, was appointed prime minister. Nagy appealed for calm and offered to introduce political reforms. Soviet troops were withdrawn to garrisons in the Hungarian countryside.

The Soviet Union hoped that this would pacify the protesters. However, Nagy proved far more liberal than they had expected. He released many political prisoners, allowed other political parties to be formed, and even formed a coalition government with some of these parties. Then, much to the horror of the Soviet leadership, the Hungarian government discussed leaving the Warsaw Pact (the organization of Eastern European communist states) and, on November 1, declared itself independent.

The Soviet response

This was a step too far for Khrushchev. A much larger force was sent into Hungary, and on November 4, around 1,000 tanks entered Budapest. Nagy sent a radio broadcast to the West pleading for help, but received no response. The Hungarian army and civilian protesters put up a brave fight, but their resistance was ruthlessly crushed. Within a few days, the fighting

was over. Around 3,000 Hungarians were killed, and perhaps 200,000 fled the country. A Soviet-backed government headed by Janos Kadar was installed. In the five years following the uprising, thousands of Hungarians were imprisoned. Nagy himself was arrested and executed in 1958.

The crushing of the Hungarian uprising dealt a severe blow to hopes of democracy in Eastern Europe. Khrushchev had clearly demonstrated that no member country would be permitted to leave the Warsaw Pact. By ignoring Nagy's plea for help, the United States had shown itself unwilling to engage in direct conflict with its superpower rival.

Soviet tanks rumble through Budapest as the uprising is ruthlessly suppressed by the Russian army.

What the papers said

With no telephonic or telegraphic communications, and with the frontier sealed by Soviet troops on the Hungarian side, no authentic independent news filtered through here today, but it seems only too likely that the (probably improvised) resistance in Budapest was crushed either late yesterday or early this morning.

The Times (London), November 6, 1956

- **SEE ALSO**
  Pages 12–13: March 6, 1953:
  Stalin Dies

- **FURTHER INFORMATION**
  📖 Books:
  Revolution in Hungary: the 1956 Budapest Uprising by Erich Lessing, Konrad Gyorgy, Francois Kejto and Nicholas Bauquet (Thames & Hudson, 2006)

  🖱 Websites:
  www.hungary1956.com/photos.htm
  For photos, clips, and Nagy's radio broadcast

Elvis Is Censored

When Elvis Presley made his third and final appearance on *The Ed Sullivan Show* in 1957, he was fast becoming one of the biggest stars in the United States. He had already enjoyed a number of hit singles, and his first film, *Love Me Tender*, was doing very well at the box office. However, not everyone approved of the young singer. Many people were worried about some of the movements made by Presley when he was performing. To a modern-day audience, he was merely wiggling his hips, but conservative Americans in the 1950s felt these movements were overtly sexual, and therefore indecent. So a remarkable decision was made by the producers of the program: They would show Elvis from the waist up only.

Television exposure

Presley had graduated from high school in 1953 in Memphis, Tennessee, and started making a name for himself as a singer on the local Country and Western music circuit. In 1955 Presley was signed by RCA, a major record label, and his records started to attract a national audience. What he needed now was more exposure. That exposure came from *The Ed Sullivan Show*.

The Ed Sullivan Show was one of the most popular programs on American television. It showcased the talents of all kinds of performers, including composers, singers, magicians, comedians, and even performing animals. Most important, the program had an eye for what was new and exciting and was the first show to feature rock and roll when Bill Hayley and the Comets appeared in August 1955. The show appealed to television executives and advertisers because it was popular with the entire family, including the new teenage market.

eye witness

This is a real decent fine boy. We've never had a pleasanter experience on our show with a big name than we've had with you. You're thoroughly all right.

Ed Sullivan

A family show

Before Elvis's controversial appearance in 1957, he had already been on *The Ed Sullivan Show* twice before. His first appearance, on September 9, 1956, had attracted a record 60 million viewers, or 80 percent of all those watching television at that particular time. There had been no complaints following either of his first two

Elvis Presley in characteristic hip-swivelling mode as he performs "Hillbilly Heartbreak" on stage in Hollywood, California, in June 1956.

performances. Nevertheless, the show's producers were concerned that Presley's performing style might alienate many viewers and harm the program's reputation as a family show.

The show itself passed without incident. Yet the producer's decision had an unexpected effect. Their crude censorship actually increased the fame of Presley and his hip-swaying antics, and the nickname "Elvis the Pelvis" firmly stuck. Despite the fact that this was to be Presley's last live television show in the United States, his career was heading straight to the top.

SEE ALSO
Pages 22–23: September 30, 1955: James Dean Dies

FURTHER INFORMATION
Books:
They Died Too Young: Elvis Presley by Melissa Hardinge (Chelsea House, 1998)
Websites:
www.elvis.com/
The official Elvis Presley website

25
MARCH
1957

The EEC Is Founded

In March 1957, representatives of six European countries met in Rome, Italy, to sign trade and atomic energy agreements. This meeting and the treaties that resulted from it would mark a permanent change in the way Europe worked, traded, and viewed itself. The two treaties, known collectively as the Treaty of Rome, were responsible for the formation of the European Economic Community (EEC) and set Europe on the road towards increasing economic and political union.

The six countries that signed the Treaty of Rome were France, Italy, Belgium, Luxembourg, the Netherlands, and West Germany. The main aim of the treaty was to bring Europe closer together and improve its prosperity, mostly by changing the way that European countries traded with each other.

Origins

The idea for the EEC was originally suggested by a French politician named Robert Schuman in 1950. Europe had been devastated by two major wars in the first half of the 20th century. Many people in Europe believed that the best way of guaranteeing peace in the future between European nations was through greater economic cooperation. World War II also marked a decisive change in world politics. The United States had emerged as the world's strongest economy, and the communist countries had formed their own trading bloc. If the countries of Europe were to compete in the world market, it made sense to work together.

The EEC came into existence on January 1, 1958. The two immediate changes were the formation of the Common Market and a customs union. These abolished all the trade quotas, tariffs, and customs barriers that had previously prevented the free movement of people, goods, services, and capital between the six countries. The six members also aimed to develop joint policies on labor, social welfare, agriculture, transportation, and foreign trade, and to work together to oppose anti-competitive practices by large companies.

 eye witness

Make no mistake about it, we are not in business, we are in politics. We are building the United States of Europe.

Walter Hallstein, one of the West German signatories of the Treaty of Rome

Representatives of six European countries sign the Treaty of Rome – actually two treaties that cover the Common Market and the European Atomic Pool.

An economic superpower

The founders of the EEC were idealists. They foresaw a time when Europe would work as one big country, which in turn would make it an economic superpower. Since 1958, there have been subsequent treaties that have altered or amended the Treaty of Rome. One change, in 1993, was to the name of the community; it is now called the European Union (EU). Over the years, many other countries have joined the community, and by January 2007 the EU had 27 member states. It is now the largest single market in the world.

The EU is often divided on many issues, and achieving consensus between member states can be very difficult. In some countries, people see the increasing political power of the EU as a threat to their status as independent nations. Despite this, many countries are keen to join the EU as its power and influence spreads ever wider.

• **FURTHER INFORMATION**
📖 Books:
World Organizations: The European Union by Jillian Powell (Franklin Watts, 2001)
🚏 Websites:
europa.eu/
The official site of the European Union

Sputnik Is Launched

The Cold War saw no direct armed conflict between the United States and the Soviet Union, but the two superpowers found other arenas in which to compete, and one of these was space. In the 1950s, both countries were eager to be the first to develop technology for the exploration of outer space with artificial satellites and, ultimately, with humans. In October 1957, the Soviet Union scored the first major victory in the space race when it launched a satellite into orbit around the Earth.

Rocket science

During World War II, the Germans had been world leaders in the field of rocket technology, used to create missiles to target enemy territories. After the war, both the United States and the Soviet Union tried to recruit German rocket scientists to help them develop rockets and missiles of their own. It soon became apparent that a rocket had the potential to leave the Earth's atmosphere and enter space. Both superpowers began developing rockets that could be fired into space, and in 1955 the United States publicly declared its plan to launch a satellite. The fact that the Soviet

eye witness

In the open West, you learn to live with the sky. It is a part of your life. But now, somehow, in some new way, the sky seemed almost alien.

Lyndon Baines Johnson, quoted in www.centennialof flight.gov/essay/SPACE FLIGHT/Sputnik/SP16.htm

A Soviet postcard commemorating the launch of the world's first artificial satellites, Sputnik 1 and, on November 3, 1957, Sputnik 2.

Union managed to do this first was both embarrassing and alarming for the United States.

The Soviets called their satellite Sputnik 1. It was nothing remarkable in itself: just a small, spherical object about 22 inches (56 centimeters) in diameter, which did nothing more than broadcast a simple radio signal as it circled the Earth. The great engineering achievement was the rocket used to place it in orbit.

Soviet technicians track the progress of Sputnik as it circles the Earth.

Sputnik's impact

Sputnik was a concern for the United States and not just because it was now clearly second in the space race. There was a defense issue here, too: if the Soviet Union could launch a satellite into space, could the Soviets launch missiles directly at U.S. cities? There was also the fear that the Soviets could use future satellites to spy on the United States. It was clear that the U.S. space program needed more investment. By the end of 1958, the United States had its own space agency, the National Aeronautics and Space Administration, or NASA.

However, the Soviet Union would continue to lead the space race for another decade. Shortly after the launch of Sputnik 1 came Sputnik 2, which carried the first space passenger, a dog called Laika. Then, in 1961, the Soviet Union put the first person into space, an army officer called Yuri Gagarin. It would not be until the moon landing of 1969 that the United States would record a decisive victory in the race to space.

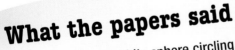

What the papers said

The Soviet Union said its sphere circling the earth had opened the way to interplanetary travel. It did not pass up the opportunity to use the launching for propaganda purposes. It said in its announcement that people now could see how "the new socialist society" had turned the boldest dreams of mankind into reality.

The New York Times, October 5, 1957

- **SEE ALSO**
  Pages 8–9: January 22, 1952:
  The First Commercial Jet Airliner

- **FURTHER INFORMATION**
  Books:
  The Race for Space: The United States and the Soviet Union Compete for the New Frontier by Betsy Kuhn (Twenty-First Century Books, 2006)
  Websites:
  www.centennialofflight.gov/essay/SPACEFLIGHT/Sputnik/SP16.htm
  For good background information and photographs

Castro Becomes Prime Minister of Cuba

On New Year's Eve 1958, President Fulgencio Batista of Cuba was forced to flee the country, along with his family and close supporters, as revolutionary forces moved toward the capital, Havana. Batista had himself siezed power in a coup in 1952. As ruler, he ignored Cuba's constitution and banned all political parties. As his rule became increasingly repressive, the Cuban people began to turn against him.

The revolutionary path

Fidel Castro, the man who was to replace Batista as leader, was born in Cuba in 1926. Bright and well educated, Castro studied law at Havana University, and although he began his career as a lawyer he became increasingly involved in politics. However, his political ambitions seemed thwarted when Batista took charge and abolished political parties. Castro became convinced that revolution was the only way to free Cuba from its new dictator.

The 1959 revolution was not the first time Castro had tried to overthrow Batista. In 1953, Castro had led an uprising that had been quickly crushed. His passionate defense during the subsequent trial raised his public profile in Cuba. Castro spent less than two years in prison, and on his release, he moved to Mexico to plan his next campaign.

Fidel Castro (standing in the center of the photograph) at his secret rebel camp near the coast. This is believed to be the only existing picture of his base. Kneeling in the foreground is Raul Castro, the leader's younger brother.

The 26th of July Movement

Castro returned in 1956 with a small band of fellow revolutionaries. After an early setback, his army, the 26th of July Movement (named after the failed uprising of 1953), slowly began to gain in strength and popular support. They launched guerrilla attacks against government forces and established underground resistance groups in the large towns and cities.

The revolutionaries also won high levels of support among the poorer, rural communities. As it became increasingly clear that Batista could not hold on to power, the Cuban army began to switch to Castro's side.

Revolution

The victorious 26th of July Movement rolled into Havana on New Year's Day 1959 amid scenes of triumph and celebration. On January 3, Castro was named Commander-in-Chief of the Cuban Armed Forces. It was soon evident that the charismatic Castro was attracting much more attention and respect than the new revolutionary government of Jose Miro Cardona. In February, Miro Cardona unexpectedly resigned and Castro became Prime Minister of Cuba.

A jubilant Fidel Castro waves to the people of Havana in January 1959.

Castro went on to become one of the longest-serving national leaders in modern history, leading his country for 47 years until his resignation in July 2006. He followed a socialist agenda, taking Cuban industry into national ownership and expanding public health, welfare, and education. His reforms made him popular among many Cubans, but he was also criticized by many others for his intolerance of political dissent, which caused many Cubans to flee from their country.

Almost from the start, Castro's Cuba was hostile to the United States and friendly to the Soviet Union. The presence of a Soviet ally in America's backyard deeply worried the United States, and after 1959, the Cold War grew a little chillier.

What the papers said

Fidel Castro yielded to the logic of circumstances yesterday and assumed the office of Premier of the Cuban Government. His original idea of letting the Cabinet Ministers [do] their respective jobs while he concentrated on the task of reorganizing the armed forces was clearly unworkable.

The New York Times, February 17, 1959

- **FURTHER INFORMATION**
- Books:
  Just the Facts Biographies: Fidel Castro (Lerner, 2006)
- Websites:
  www.npr.org/templates/story/story.php?storyId =5598311
  For a timeline and recordings of Castro's speeches

  news.bbc.co.uk/1/hi/world/americas/ country_profiles/1203299.stm
  Information on and history of Cuba

Barbie Is Launched

In March 1959, the toy manufacturer Mattel unveiled a new product at the American Toy Fair in New York City. It was a plastic doll called Barbie. The doll was 11.5 inches (29 centimeters) long and came dressed in a black-and-white striped bathing suit. What made Barbie different from other dolls was that, rather than being a baby, she was a girl in her late teens. The buyers at the fair were generally unimpressed. No one, including the directors of Mattel, could have predicted what an extraordinary success Barbie would turn out to be.

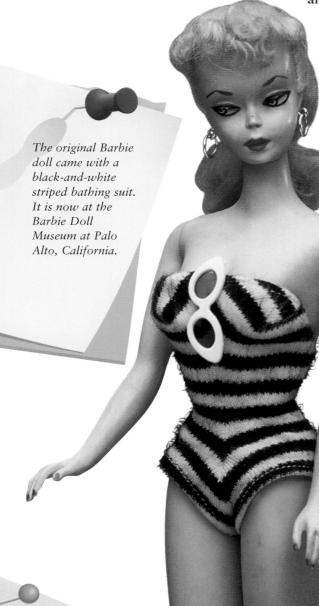

The original Barbie doll came with a black-and-white striped bathing suit. It is now at the Barbie Doll Museum at Palo Alto, California.

A new kind of doll

The Barbie doll was invented by a woman named Ruth Handler who, along with her husband Elliot and friend Harold Matson, had founded Mattel in 1945. Ruth got her inspiration for Barbie from watching her daughter, Barbara, playing with cut-out paper dolls and dressing them in cut-out clothes. Ruth realized that there was no toy equivalent of her daughter's creations – all the dolls on the market were modeled on babies. There were no aspirational dolls out there for little girls to live out their fantasies with. She took the idea to the board of Mattel, but they did not think the idea would work. Ruth was not to be discouraged. On a trip to Switzerland she spotted a German doll called Lilli, which was similar to her own idea. Ruth persuaded Mattel to buy the rights for an American version of Lilli and set about improving it. Dressing the doll in different outfits would be a vital part of its appeal, so the clothes had to be good. Ruth hired the fashion designer Charlotte Johnson to design the costumes. The toy had to be affordable, too, so Mattel arranged to manufacture it in China, where production costs were lower. Finally, the doll needed a name, and there was only one possibility: Barbie, the nickname of Ruth's daughter.

Ruth Handler, co-founder of toy manufacturer Mattel, was the driving force behind Barbie.

⊙ **eye** witness

I wouldn't walk around the house like that. I don't like that influence on my little girl. If only they would let children remain young a little longer.... It's hard enough to raise a lady these days without undue moral pressures.

A concerned mother thinks that the new Barbie doll is unsuitable for children. Quoted from www.honors.umd.edu/HONR269J/projects/wolf.html

Billion-seller Barbie

The buyers at the toy fair may have been unmoved, but the general public was extremely taken with the new toy. In the first year, Mattel sold 351,000 dolls at $3 each. Demand was so high that Mattel had difficulty in fulfilling all the orders. That is not to say that everyone liked the new doll. Some parents worried that it encouraged their daughters to grow up too fast. More recently, Barbie's extremely slender build has been criticized for promoting an unrealistic body shape for women, which might lead some girls to try to lose weight to look like her. In 1997, Barbie was redesigned with a wider waist.

Despite the occasional controversy, the doll sold, and continues to sell well. The Barbie range has been extended to include a male equivalent, Ken, and several others. To date, over half a billion Barbie dolls have been sold. Total sales across the whole range amount to over a billion. The doll launched at the 1959 American Toy Fair has become a superstar.

- **SEE ALSO**
  Pages 20–21: April 15, 1955: The McDonald's Franchise Begins

- **FURTHER INFORMATION**
  📖 Books:
  Inventors and Creators: Ruth Handler: Creator of Barbie by Cynthia Mines (KidHaven Press, 2007)
  ⌐ Websites:
  www.mattel.com/About_Us/History/mattel_history.pdf
  For a timeline of Mattel's history

15 OCTOBER 1951

I Love Lucy Debuts on TV

October 15, 1951 seemed like just another Monday night. At 9 P.M. (Eastern time), television viewers tuned in to a new show—a half-hour situation comedy called *I Love Lucy*. No one realized that *I Love Lucy* would become one of the most popular shows in TV history and that its star, Lucille Ball, would become one of the most beloved performers.

The cast of I Love Lucy. *From left: Lucille Ball, Vivian Vance (Ethel), Desi Arnaz, and William Frawley (Fred).*

Family Comedy with a Twist

I Love Lucy centered around a housewife named Lucy Ricardo (played by Ball) and her husband, a Cuban singer named Ricky Ricardo, played by Ball's real-life husband, Desi Arnaz. The Ricardos live in a New York City apartment. Their landlords and best friends are Fred and Ethel Mertz.

During the 1950s, many sitcoms were about marriages and families. *I Love Lucy* was different because Lucy wanted more out of life than just being a housewife. She wants to break into show business, like Ricky. Unfortunately, she is not very talented. In addition, aided by Ethel, Lucy often comes up with crazy schemes and gets into ridiculous situations. Viewers tuned in week after week to see what Lucy would do next. In one episode, she films a commercial for a product called Vitameatavegamin. She does not know that it contains a great deal of alcohol, so she becomes more and more drunk as the day goes on. In another episode, Lucy and Ethel go to work

◉ eye witness

The evening that *I Love Lucy* first went on the air, the director and his wife invited us all to have dinner and watch the premiere.... We had seen the show at the filming, so there wasn't much laughter. But Vivian's husband ... who hadn't been at the filming, was laughing so hard he almost fell out of his chair, which we hoped was a good omen.

Madelyn Pugh Davis and Bob Carroll, *I Love Lucy* writers, looking back on the night of October 15, 1951

in a candy factory, wrapping the candy as it goes by on a conveyor belt. But the pace gets quicker and quicker and the women can't keep up, winding up stuffing candy in their mouths, blouses, and hats.

During its first season, 1951–1952, *I Love Lucy* was the third most popular show on television. It then soared to the top and for four years of its six-year run was the most popular show on TV. One of the show's largest audiences came on January 19, 1953, when 44 million people tuned in to watch Lucy give birth to a son, Little Ricky.

Lasting Legacy

I Love Lucy was significant in many ways beyond its popularity. It was one of the first shows whose main star was a woman and one of the first to star a member of a minority group. The network had been reluctant to hire Arnaz, fearing that the public was not ready to accept a Latin leading man.

The show also introduced a new production process. It was filmed before a live studio audience using high-quality 35mm film and three cameras instead of just one. This captured the spontaneity of a live performance with lasting film quality. The filming technique became common throughout the television industry.

After six years and 181 episodes, *I Love Lucy* ended its regular run. For the next three years, the stars appeared in 13 one-hour episodes, called *The Lucille Ball–Desi Arnaz Show*. To millions of viewers, Lucy and Ricky live on in reruns and syndication. The show is still shown around the world in dozens of languages and is regularly named one of the greatest TV shows in history.

Lucy and Ethel cross rooftops on a wobbly plank during a scene from the show.

- **SEE ALSO**
Pages 38–39: March 9, 1959: Barbie Is Launched

- **FURTHER INFORMATION**
- Books:
  I Love Lucy: The Complete Picture History of the Most Popular TV Show Ever by Michael McClay (Warner Books, 1995)
- Websites:
  www.lucy-desi.com
  The website of the Lucille Ball–Desi Arnaz Center in Jamestown, NY

School Segregation Declared Unconstitutional

Linda Brown was an African-American third grader from Topeka, Kansas. Even though there was an elementary school only seven blocks from her house, she could not go there because the school was for white students only. Instead, Linda had to walk six blocks through a dangerous train yard to catch a bus that took her to a school for black students.

Separate but Equal?

In the early 1950s, in parts of the United States—especially in the South—blacks were forced to use separate facilities, such as parks, beaches, and restaurants, as well as schools. These were rarely the equal of the facilities enjoyed by whites.

Leaders of the NAACP (the National Association for the Advancement of Colored People) decided to use the case of Linda Brown to confront the system. They asked Oliver Brown, Linda's father, to try to enroll her in the local white school. When the school turned her away, Brown filed a lawsuit against the Topeka Board of Education. After a local court ruled in favor of the board, the case was appealed to the Supreme Court.

In the case of *Brown* v. *Board of Education of Topeka*, the chief counsel for the NAACP was Thurgood Marshall, a young African-American lawyer. Marshall argued that school segregation violated the Fourteenth Amendment to the U.S. Constitution, which requires that all U.S. citizens be treated the same, regardless of race.

Linda Brown (front, center) sits in class at the black-only Monroe Elementary School in Topeka, Kansas.

A Victory for Equal Rights

On May 17, 1954, the Supreme Court issued its unanimous 9–0 ruling, declaring that it was unconstitutional to create separate schools for children based on race. Chief Justice Earl Warren read the decision to the courtroom. "We come then to the question presented," he stated. "Does

Thurgood Marshall (center) speaks to reporters following the Supreme Court ruling.

segregation of children in public schools solely on the basis of race, even though the physical facilities and other 'tangible' factors may be equal, deprive the children of the minority group of equal educational opportunities? We believe that it does."

The decision was a victory for equal rights, but change did not come overnight. In 1955, the Supreme Court ordered federal district courts to desegregate the schools with "all deliberate speed." However, many southern states delayed and resisted desegregation for years. The struggle for full equal rights in education—and the rest of society—would continue well into the 1960s.

- **SEE ALSO**
  Pages 24–25: December 1, 1955:
  Rosa Parks Refuses to Change Seats

- **FURTHER INFORMATION**
  📖 Books:
  Brown v. Board of Education by Marty Gitlin (ABDO Publishing Company, 2007)
  Remember: The Journey to School Integration by Toni Morrison (Houghton Mifflin, 2004)
  Websites:
  www.nps.gov/brvb
  The *Brown* v. *Board of Education* National Historic Site in Topeka, Kansas

What the papers said

The Supreme Court's resolution yesterday ... affords all Americans an occasion for pride and gratification. The decision will prove, we are sure ... a profoundly healthy and healing one.... It will bring an end to a painful disparity between American principles and American practice.

Washington, DC *Post & Times-Herald,* May 18, 1954

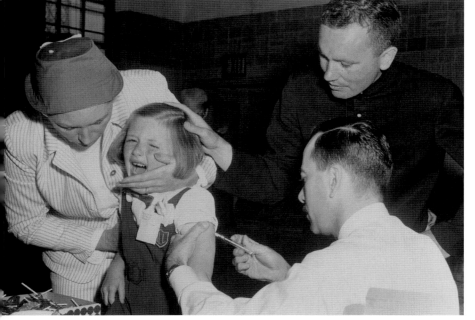

12
APRIL

1955

Polio Vaccine Declared Effective

In April 1954, children lined up at the Franklin Sherman Elementary School in McLean, Virginia, to receive an experimental vaccine to prevent polio. They were the first in the United States to receive the vaccine. Soon, 1.8 million students in 44 states across the country were being tested as well. They were called "Polio Pioneers" and were part of the largest experiment of its kind in medical history, undertaken to find a way to prevent a terrible illness that had reached epidemic levels around the world. One year later, on April 12, 1955, the developers of the vaccine announced that it was safe and effective. Churches rang their bells and fire stations blew their sirens in celebration at the news that children would no longer be stricken by the dreaded disease.

A devastating disease

Polio (or poliomyelitis) is a disease caused by a virus that attacks nerve cells and the central nervous system, causing muscles to weaken. The result can be paralysis and even death. The disease, which is contagious, usually strikes children, but adults can also be affected. Franklin D. Roosevelt, for example, came down with polio in 1921 when he was 39 years old. Polio had been around for many years, but it reached frightening levels in the 1950s. In 1952 alone, 57,628 cases were reported in the United States. Most of them were children. Families were often forced to separate, with patients taken away and isolated from the general public.

A number of research teams tried to develop a vaccine for polio. A vaccine is a substance containing a very weak or small amount of a virus. If the human body is exposed to this, it produces antibodies—substances that resist or kill the virus. The body will then be able to fight off the disease if it is later exposed to the virus. Polio was tricky to work with because there are 125 different strains of the virus

A child from Malverne, New York, receives the newly developed polio vaccine in May 1955.

that fall into three basic types. Dr. Jonas Salk, working at the Virus Research Laboratory of the University of Pittsburgh, knew that to be effective, a polio vaccine had to include all three types.

Using a number of methods discovered by other researchers, Salk was able to grow the virus in the lab and kill it using the chemical formaldehyde, leaving enough of the virus intact to still produce antibodies. In 1952, he began testing the vaccine on small groups of volunteers, including himself, his wife, and his three sons. In 1954, widespread testing began.

Dr. Jonas Salk, discoverer of the polio vaccine, at work in his laboratory in Pittsburgh.

A great success

On April 12, 1955, Dr. Thomas Francis, Jr.—Salk's associate, who conducted the vaccine trials— announced that the vaccine was safe and effective. The vaccine was licensed and made available to the public immediately. It was a great success. In 1955, there were 28,985 U.S. cases of polio; in 1957, the figure had dropped to just 5,894. Polio is now rare in the United States and most of the world. An effort is under way to eliminate it worldwide using widespread vaccination programs.

⊙ eye witness

I walked into the isolation ward.... No one was allowed in except the doctors and nurses, and they wore masks. My parents stood outside ... bravely waving and blowing kisses ...

Peg Kehret, who was diagnosed with polio in 1948 and paralyzed for nine months before recovering

• SEE ALSO
Pages 18–19: December 23, 1954: The First Organ Transplant

• FURTHER INFORMATION
📖 Books:
Jonas Salk: Beyond the Microscope by Victoria Sherrow (Chelsea House Publications, 2008)
🖱 Websites:
americanhistory.si.edu/polio/index.htm
A Smithsonian Institution website with information about polio and the fight to prevent it.

People of the Decade

Marlon Brando
(1924–2004)
Marlon Brando was arguably the most exciting movie actor of the 1950s. He was one of the greatest early exponents of the technique known as method acting, in which the actor attempts to identify with the emotions of the character being played. Brando gave electrifying performances in films such as *A Streetcar Named Desire* (1951), *The Wild One* (1953), and *On the Waterfront* (1954), for which he won an Oscar. He was an inspiration for many young actors, including James Dean and Jack Nicholson, and his influence continues to this day.

Sir Winston Churchill
(1874–1965)
Britain's charismatic war leader returned as prime minister in 1951 and continued in office until his resignation in 1955. He was also a prolific painter and author, receiving the Nobel Prize for Literature in 1953. In that year he was also knighted by the newly crowned Queen Elizabeth II. Churchill was an early supporter of closer ties with Europe, but also sought to maintain a special relationship with the United States.

Albert Einstein
(1879–1955)
The year 1955 witnessed the death of one of the world's greatest scientists. So famous was he that most ordinary people had not only heard of him but would recognize a picture of him, too. In 1905, Einstein proposed his special theory of relativity, followed ten years later by his general theory of relativity. These two towering achievements transformed forever the way physicists looked at the universe. He received the Nobel Prize in Physics for his work in 1921.

Dwight D. Eisenhower
(1890–1969)
Eisenhower was the 34th president of the United States. During World War II he had been Supreme Commander of the Allied Troops invading France and was later the Supreme Commander of the newly formed NATO. Nominated by the Republican Party, he was elected president in 1952 and remained in office until 1961.

Charles de Gaulle
(1890–1970)
In 1958, Charles de Gaulle, wartime leader of the Free French and first postwar leader of France, became prime minister again, following the political turmoil that resulted from the uprising in the French colony of Algiers. While in office, de Gaulle drafted a new constitution, which the French people voted to accept, and he was made president in 1959.

Pope John XXIII
(1881–1963)
Following the death of Pope Pius XII in 1958, Cardinal Angelo Roncalli was elected pope and became the leader of the Roman Catholic Church. Taking the name John XXIII, he began his papacy by visiting hospitals and prisons – unheard of behavior for a pope. This, along with his gentle and smiling demeanor, made him extremely popular. He would go on to introduce major reforms to the Catholic Church, bringing the congregation into closer participation with church services and improving relations with other religions.

Harold Macmillan
(1894–1986)
Harold Macmillan was an effective member of Britain's Conservative administration of the 1950s, occupying a number of cabinet positions before taking over as prime minister in 1956 when Anthony Eden stepped down after the Suez Crisis. Macmillan was initially a lucky Prime Minister. The British economy was improving and people generally felt better about life. He won the general election of 1959 and was popular enough to earn the nickname Supermac. He resigned in 1963 due to ill health, possibly made worse by a scandal that severely damaged his government.

J. R. R. Tolkien
(1892–1973)
John Ronald Reuel Tolkien was a professor of Anglo-Saxon at Oxford University and a prolific writer. His most famous work, *The Lord of the Rings*, was published in three volumes between 1954 and 1955. It began as a sequel to his earlier work, *The Hobbit*, but became a much larger story. *The Lord of the Rings* is a fantasy epic peopled with creatures such as hobbits, elves, dwarves, and orcs, as well as humans. It has become one of the most popular books in 20th-century literature.

Harry S. Truman
(1884–1972)
Harry S. Truman became the 33rd president of the United States in 1945, following the death in office of his predecessor, Franklin D. Roosevelt. Truman took over just as World War II was ending and the Cold War was starting to loom. He was re-elected president in 1948. In 1950, Truman intervened as North Korea invaded South Korea. He sent in troops in support of South Korea. Meanwhile, at home, Truman's administration came under attack as Joseph McCarthy began his anti-communist witch hunts, claiming the government itself was harboring enemies of the state.

Glossary

administration A government.

aspirational Describing an object that inspires a person toward self-improvement.

Bolshevik A communist political party in Russia.

ceasefire An agreement between opposing sides in a conflict that they will stop fighting, usually to enable peace talks to take place.

Central Committee In the Soviet Union the part of the government that was responsible for party policy.

cinder race track During the 1950s athletic tracks were constructed from cinder which came from cooled lava and provided grip on the running surface.

civil rights The rights that all citizens of a society are supposed to enjoy, such as the right to vote or the right to receive fair treatment under the law.

commercial air travel The use of air transportation by ordinary civilians or commercial companies, as distinct from military air transport.

communist A believer in state control of the economy and the equal distribution of wealth.

conveyor belt A moving belt that transports objects from place to place.

destalinization The move away from Stalin's policies, and the introduction of a less ruthless style of government, by the leaders of the Soviet Union.

discrimination The unfair treatment of a person or group, usually because of prejudice about, for example, their race, ethnic group, religion, or sexuality.

epidemic A fast-spreading disease.

ideology A system of beliefs and ideas that form the basis for a political philosophy or program.

franchise An agreement to sell a company's products exclusively in a particular area or to operate a business that carries that company's name.

guerrilla A member of an independent fighting force usually with some political aim such as the overthrow of a government.

Marx, Karl A German political philosopher (1818–1883) whose ideas inspired, among others, communist revolutionaries in Russia and, later, China.

NATO The North Atlantic Treaty Organization is a military alliance established in 1949 by the United States and a number of Western European countries to promote collective security during the Cold War.

organ transplant The transfer of an organ (such as a heart, kidney, or lung) from one person to another.

polio A serious infectious disease, caused by a virus, that affects the brain and spinal cord, sometimes leading to paralysis, muscle wasting, and death; short for poliomyelitis.

Republican Party One of the two main political parties in the United States. The other main party is the Democratic Party.

revolution The overthrow of a government or political system.

revolutionary A person who takes an active role in a revolution.

Roman Catholic Church A Christian Church that has a pope as its head and is administered from the Vatican City in Rome.

satellite An object in orbit around another object in space. For example, the Moon is a satellite of Earth.

Secretary of State The U.S. government official who is in charge of foreign policy.

segregation The practice of keeping groups—especially ethnic, racial, religious, or gender groups—separate through the use of separate schools, transportation, housing, and other facilities.

situation comedy A television comedy series featuring the same characters each week; often called a sitcom.

sovereignty The authority to rule over a state.

Soviet Union Also known as the USSR (Union of Soviet Socialist Republics), a country formed from the territories of the Russian Empire in 1917, which lasted until 1991.

socialist Relating to, or belief in, a political system in which wealth is shared equally between people, and the main industries and trade are controlled by the government.

space race The Cold War-inspired competition between the United States and the Soviet Union, which lasted from around 1957 to 1975, to be the first to explore outer space with artificial satellites and, later, with humans.

superpowers An extremely powerful nation with greater political, economic, or military power than most other nations. The term was used to describe the United States and the Soviet Union during the Cold War period.

unconstitutional Against the principles set out in a country's constitution. A constitution is a written statement containing the basic laws or principles by which a country is governed.

USSR *see* Soviet Union

United Nations An organization of nations, formed in 1945, to promote peace, security, and international cooperation.

vaccine A substance containing dead or weakened organisms of the kind that cause a disease, which is administered to stimulate a person's immune system to produce antibodies against that disease.

witch-hunt A systematic campaign directed against people who hold different views. The term refers back to the time when women were put to death in the belief that they were witches.

Index